# Enough.

## Helen Roseveare

CHRISTIAN
**FOCUS**

**10** Publishing

Copyright © Helen Roseveare 2011

ISBN 978-1-84550-751-0

10 9 8 7 6 5 4

Published in 2011
Reprinted twice in 2011, 2012 and once in 2013
by
Christian Focus Publications, Ltd
Geanies House, Fearn,
Ross-shire, IV20 1TW, Scotland
www.christianfocus.com
with
10ofthose.com
Common Bank Industrial Estate,
Ackhurst Road, Chorley PR7 1NH, England

Cover design by Daniel van Straaten

Printed by Nørhaven, Denmark

# CONTENTS

# Prologue

*'Enough's enough!'*
My father's strict voice cut through the noise the three of us children were making as we rough-housed together. Silence fell at once – Father was being disturbed by our noise.

'Helen, you've had *enough*.'

My mother's gentle voice made me draw my hand back, as I stretched out for another chocolate biscuit. Her tone of voice said: 'You don't need another; your hunger has been satisfied. To take another is greed.'

'Have I cut off *enough*?' queried the nervous hairdresser, seeking to please both her young client's request to 'cut it short' and Mother's warning not to cut it too short!

Waiting anxiously for the results of recent exams to go up, everyone was poised, with eyes fixed on the boards. And then the excited whistles, laughs and exclamation of joy (mixed with the tears of those who had not made the necessary grades). 'I've *enough*!' *Enough* to make it possible to go on to the next year's studies – or to gain the coveted place at the chosen university.

Mother's gentle whispered 'FHB!' to her three excited children one evening. Father had come home with unexpected guests and Mother was afraid the food prepared for the evening meal would not be *enough* for everyone to have all they might wish. So it was 'Family Hold Back'!

Being interviewed before the senior members of the mission organisation WEC International[1] to determine whether I was a suitable candidate for acceptance into their missionary family, I nervously answered each

---

1    WEC International is an international movement committed to the gospel of Jesus Christ, aiming to reach people and to plant churches in over 70 countries in the world.

question put to me and watched their faces, trying to see if my answers satisfied them. I had been at the mission's headquarters for five months, taking part in the daily life of the family each day – sometimes being allotted to the kitchen, at other times to the laundry or to general household duties, and every morning at the daily prayer session. Had I shown *enough* dedication, *enough* maturity, *enough* willingness to do anything asked of me, to be accepted into the family?

A year later, all my gathered possessions were packed into tea-chests and duly labelled, I had received all the necessary 'jabs' (inoculations and vaccinations) and was waiting for the travel documents and tickets. Would I have *enough* to pay for the journey?

One could go on and on. Would my stamina be *enough* in Congo's heat to work 18 hours a day? Would my brain be resilient *enough* to learn the Swahili language? Even, dare I say it, would my love for the Lord Jesus be *enough* to take me through the initial culture shock and loneliness? Oddly enough, I never even asked any of these questions at the time. But I expect my dear mother pondered them and wondered if I could stand up to all the new stresses and difficulties. Had her upbringing of her children been *enough* to prepare them for all the world would throw at them?

Years later, faced with the horror of captivity in the civil war of the sixties, filled with fear at the ferocity of our captors and the atrocities we had to witness, had I *enough* resilience, had I *enough* faith, to trust God absolutely? To be so sure of his almighty power and omnipotence, as to be able to rest in him, even when the world seemed to be falling apart? And then, in the night that I was first taken captive, feeling desperately alone and wondering where God was in the midst of all the evil, being conscious of his quiet voice into my heart, 'Can you thank me?' and feeling, 'No, God, I can't possibly. This is all too awful.' And then realising that what he was actually saying to me was, 'Can you thank me for trusting *you* with this experience?' As I caught the import of his words, 'I thought you knew me well *enough*, to trust me even when you couldn't understand the outcome or the reason', I was overwhelmed at the privilege of being trusted by him, to go through whatever was coming next, because it was all part of his perfect plan. He didn't have to explain to me the why and wherefore of that plan.

Later still, because of the needs of my frail mother and also my own physical needs, I had to leave Congo – and the people and work that I loved – and come back to the UK. I found it desperately difficult to come to terms with the fact that God (not the mission, nor my mother) had called me home to lead me into a new ministry. The same question came back at me with renewed vigour: 'Can you thank me?' It took nearly eight years before I could honestly thank him for trusting me with this change of direction. The work was hard and often very lonely, travelling endlessly, living out of a suitcase, relating to a new group of people every day. Eventually there came a day when I felt like telling our patient loving heavenly Father, 'I've had *enough*!' But his quiet reply, as ever, 'Can you not thank me for trusting you with this task, even if I never tell you why?'

Ten different uses of the same English word 'enough' with several different nuances. It is a word that might well be translated by many different words or phrases – but I do believe that they can all be summed up in the one word: 'sufficiency'.

Just as there are many ways of using the word 'enough' in our everyday lives, so there are many ways of understanding this in our spiritual lives. There is a wonderful truth that God has *enough* to supply all our needs. *Enough* for salvation, *enough* for forgiveness, *enough* to overcome temptations, *enough* to persevere in adversities, *enough* to calm our fears and anxieties. *Enough* grace, *enough* love, *enough* power. His supply is sufficient to meet not only all our needs, but the needs of everyone else in the world, now and at all times. This is summed up in the promise: 'My grace is sufficient for you' (2 Cor. 12:9). That is to say, it is *enough*. By his grace we have everything we need to live the life he has planned for us, everything we need to live a life that is pleasing to him.

Sufficient grace – that means there is always *enough* for all our needs. This thought is summed up in Graham Hobson's words

> Grace sufficient he'll provide you,
> Grace in just the way you need;
> Grace to save you, grace to guide you,
> Grace from sin to keep you freed;
> Grace that you may stand unmoving,
> Grace in conflict to succeed;
> Grace sufficient, always proving
> His is wondrous grace indeed.

# 1

# Enough
# for Salvation

---

Am I sure that there is no other way
to peace of heart
than that of trusting in the death and
resurrection
of our Lord Jesus Christ?

*'Salvation is found in no-one else,*
*for there is no other Name under heaven*
*given to men by which we must be saved.'*

Acts 4:12

---

# | 1 |

# Enough
# for Salvation

Going to university in the closing months of World War Two, having grown up as a church-goer, I was suddenly unsure. Could I really believe in a God who had been unable to settle the affairs of nations except by a terrible war? – friends who had lost family members, the appalling destruction of cities, the shortage of food. So many questions on all sides. If there was a God, why hadn't he stepped in to stop the carnage?

Having spent seven years in a Church of England boarding school where church attendance was obligatory and everyone on staff gave at least the outward appearance of being part of the system, I had not questioned the religious input. But now? I was free to think, and come to my own conclusions. Was it all a sham? A pretence? Could I honestly believe in the existence of such a God? Would it be more honest to say I was uncertain, even if I wouldn't go as far as saying I did not believe in the existence of God?

But to say there is no God landed me in an awful quandary. If there is no God, who has the authority to say what is right and wrong? If each is responsible for making their own decision, would not chaos reign? Whether one drove on the right or the left of the road, each one to decide what they liked? Disaster! And what if my decision about God was wrong? Would it not be better to keep a foot in each camp, in case I was wrong? Keep on going to church at least once each Sunday, but leave him out of my reckoning the rest of the time?

I started going to other meetings such as Communist Party meetings, learning about

Dialectical Materialism; also meetings of Christian Scientists – that quickly seemed neither Christian nor scientific! In my search for the truth, I found only loneliness and fear. I probably did not realise it but I must have been searching for a God big enough to answer all my longings, big enough to solve all the problems, big enough to make sense of the world we lived in, with all its insecurities and uncertainties.

Then I met up with Christian girls in the college Christian Union. They were different – kind, thoughtful, generous with their friendship, willing to give time to help others find their way around. They really were different – they were polite, courteous, and quietly self-sufficient without being arrogant. They had a peace about them that I found very intriguing. Eventually one of them invited me to go to church with her one Sunday evening.

We cycled to the 8.00 pm service at a central church in Cambridge. At least out of courtesy, even if with no particular interest, I had agreed to go along with them. And for the first time in my life I heard the simple, straight gospel – that Jesus Christ, God's beloved son, died on the cross at Calvary for my sins. The preacher read a verse from Paul's first letter to Timothy. The friend who had taken me opened her Bible and pointed the verse out to me: 'There is one God, and one mediator between God and men, the man Christ Jesus; who gave himself a ransom for all' (1 Tim. 2:5-6 AV) in the old Authorized Version (we had no other version at that time).

I read and re-read the verse, hardly listening to the rest of the sermon. There was a truth there that I wanted desperately to believe. It seemed too good to be true! No other mediator was needed. No other method to be forgiven, than to believe that Jesus was my ransom. He died instead of me, where I deserved to die. He loved me so much that he was willing to die for me. He loved me enough to die for me! Could it really be as simple as that?

In the weeks ahead, throughout that Christmas term, I started going to Bible studies and prayer meetings every week. I had no other friends really, apart from those Christian Union girls and I was drawn to them. But there were so many questions in my mind. I had gone regularly to the confessional (in a high Anglo-Catholic church, pastored by a Franciscan monk) and to the mass each Sunday. Which way was right? Logically, they couldn't both be right. The way of following rules and regulations, giving obedience to the system, was the easiest and seemed the safest – but I knew that this was not satisfying some inner need. It was not giving me the peace and the joy that I longed for. Could the other way be right? But to follow the way of those Christian Union girls I would have to deliberately give up the past way – which, of course, I had already half-done! But I was afraid to break completely from the past. What if I was wrong?

In the Christmas holidays, I went to a Christian house party organised by my new friends – all Christian young women, training to be leaders on a Christian holiday for girls the following summer. They were all praying for me as they all knew that I was not a Christian – only I did not know this fact! I thought I was a Christian – by my regular church attendance and efforts to be good. The teaching through the week was clear and Biblical. We were led through a study of Genesis and then through Paul's letter to the Romans. During the last day, the fight in my heart was almost palpable. I wanted their assurance, their knowledge of God as their Saviour, their peace – but I dreaded the possibility of being wrong and forfeiting all the past.

There was an elderly lady at the house party, little Miss Candy. I went to see her to ask her help – how could I be sure?

'What is your difficulty?' she asked me.

'In the Bible, when Jesus gave the bread and wine to his disciples at the Last Supper, he said, 'This is my body' and 'This is my blood' – but you people don't believe this!'

Miss Candy asked me to go to the locker by her bedside and bring her the photo that was there. As I gave it to her she said, 'This is my father.'

I knew at once what she was saying. Her father had been dead for many years. The photo reminded her of her father. Likewise the bread and wine were to be reminders to us of what Jesus had done for us on the cross.

I was half persuaded but still uncertain. At supper that evening, an altercation broke out at the table and I lost my temper. Ashamed,

I rushed out and upstairs to the dormitory. Throwing myself on my bed, I cried, 'God, if there is a God, please make yourself known to me – now!' Looking up through my tears, I saw a text printed on the wall above me and I read, 'Be still! And know that I am...' (The last word had been washed away by leaking rain!) God had spoken to me. I was awed.

'Be still! Stop all your struggling and fearing and arguing and know that I am God! I love you, I died for you. Trust me and stop being unbelieving.'

And I knew. God himself had spoken – and peace poured into my heart. God so loved me that he had died for me. What love! And I believe in that wonderful sacred moment, I truly fell in love with Jesus, my Lord and my Saviour. Did I have to do anything else? No. It was indeed enough. He had paid the whole price for my sins. It was all of grace. There was nothing I had to do, just to thank him with all my heart. His death was sufficient for everyone who believed and accepted his death instead of them. Wonderful Saviour!

Here is love, vast as the ocean,
Loving-kindness as the flood,

When the Prince of Life, our Ransom,
Shed for us His precious blood.
Who His love will not remember?
Who can cease to sing His praise?
He can never be forgotten
Throughout Heav'n's eternal days.

On the mount of crucifixion
Fountains opened deep and wide;
Through the flood gates of God's mercy
Flowed a vast and gracious tide.
Grace and love, like mighty rivers,
Poured incessant from above,
And Heav'n's peace and perfect justice
Kissed a guilty world in love.

William Rees (1802-1883)

# 2

# Enough
# for Assurance

---

**Can there be any other way to deal with
guilt and sorrow?
Do I have to DO 'something' more than
just believe?**

*'If you confess with your mouth, "Jesus is Lord,"
and believe in your heart that God
raised Him from the dead,
you will be saved.'*

Romans 10:9, 10

---

# | 2 |

# Enough
# for Assurance

When I came home from Congo on my first furlough in 1958, I was not totally sure about going back again. (Furlough is a break from missionary work for rest and visits to family, friends and supporting churches.) Despite loving the people and the work, there was a nagging feeling that 'if I was married' there would be someone else to make decisions, to carry the final responsibility in all aspects of the work. I probably did not actually want 'to be married' – that is, to have a husband –just to have a man about the place!

I got a job as a junior houseman in a hospital in London, to bring my medical knowledge and skills up to a higher standard. Not unnaturally, I became friendly with the other doctors with whom I was working – and I began to think that one of them could easily be called to go out to serve God in Congo! As my six months at that hospital began to slip by, I felt frustrated that there was no sign of anyone wanting to work with me in the remote region on the equator – without proper equipment, with no electricity and no running water!

So I took the drastic step of resigning from my mission, as I felt that my insistence that I was called to be a missionary was a definite handicap preventing anyone becoming attached to me as a life partner! Then I had no peace. I knew I had acted rashly and without seeking any guidance from God. In July of that year, I went to the Keswick Convention[1] – and there God graciously renewed my call to serve him, even if it meant staying single, even if

---

1    An annual gathering of Christians in Keswick, Cumbria.

it meant sticking it out in Congo with all its frustrating limitations. At the second morning meeting on the second day of the convention, the speaker spoke from Hebrews 4:14-16 and he underlined the thought, 'Let us come boldly unto the throne of grace, that we may obtain mercy and find grace to help in time of need' (Heb. 4:16 AV).

I needed his mercy to forgive me for having rejected his call (even if for only a short time), and I would need his grace daily to go back to what I knew was a hard spot. But his promise was clear – come to him, ask him, take from him all that is needed.

I responded to the message that morning – but only in part. I knew that as I repented of my wilfulness, God was so gracious that he forgave me my sinfulness but somehow I could not forgive myself. I seemed to think that I had forfeited the right to be forgiven. My actions had been deliberate. The fact that I had never deserved God's forgiveness in the first place – a fact that I knew perfectly well – did not seem to help me find peace at that moment in time.

I went back to Congo in 1960. I served again at Nebobongo. I survived the turmoil and fears of the tensions of Independence. I coped with the shortages and never-ending frustrations in every area of the work. But throughout those four years (1960–64), even though I was doing what I ought to do, teaching what I ought to teach, yet I had no real peace in my heart or joy at serving the Master. Somewhere along the line, I believed that I had first to atone for my actions during furlough. I believed I had to do something (or suffer something) to deserve to be forgiven even though, at the same time, I knew that he had forgiven me. How contrary we can be! As I will mention in the next chapter, he had spoken to me so clearly, during a spell of time in hospital during that furlough (1958–60) – and I had accepted his forgiveness and a renewal of his call to me to be his servant in Congo, at Nebobongo, and yet there remained this nagging fear, prompted by the fact that I could not fully forgive myself.

Then the civil war broke over us and I was captured by rebel soldiers. Five months were to follow with wickedness and cruelty all around us. Sleepless nights, constantly being watched, threatened with unspeakable atrocities, seeing others suffer. Then the night when I myself was taken by these

wicked men and 'suffered' at their hands –
the euphemism that we all used to speak of
their misuse of women. In my heart, I cried
out to God for his protection.

And God, in his loving mercy, spoke peace
into my heart. I almost felt his loving arms
around me. 'Twenty years ago, you asked me
for the privilege of being a missionary. This is
it. Don't you want it?'

No, I didn't want it! And yet, I desperately
wanted God's comfort.

'Can you thank me for trusting you with
this, even if I never tell you why?'

Could this really be the voice of God himself – him trusting me, rather than me trusting him? After the four years of struggle in
my heart to truly accept and trust in his forgiveness of me, this was extraordinary!

And a verse of Scripture came into my
mind: 'How is it to your credit if you receive
a beating for doing wrong and endure it?
But if you suffer for doing good and you
endure it, this is commendable before
God' (1 Pet. 2:20). Or, as it is written in the
Authorised Version, which I knew by heart,
'What glory is it, if, when you are buffeted
for your faults, you shall take it patiently?

But if, when you do well and suffer for it, you take it patiently, this is acceptable with God' (1 Pet. 2:20 AV).

It was as though a curtain was taken away from my mind. Immediately, I knew the fact of his wonderful, unchanging love, the full peace of his forgiveness. I realised that I could do nothing to deserve or merit his forgiveness – he had done all that could be done when he died on the cross at Calvary, when he bore my sins (*all* my sin, not a part) on his body on the tree. There was nothing more to be done. Just to believe and trust and accept. Just being humble enough to admit my failure, my sin, and ask his forgiveness.

> 'Salvation is found in no one else, for there is no other name under heaven given to men, by which we must be saved' (Acts 4:12).

His name – the name above all names. The name his Father gave him – Jesus!

All we need for peace, forgiveness, assurance, salvation – all is in the name of Jesus. It is enough in *all* circumstances. When Peter and John met the lame man at the Gate Beautiful and he asked them for money, Peter replied, 'Silver or gold I do not have, but what I have I give you. In the name of Jesus Christ of Nazareth, walk' (Acts 3:6). And the man, who had been lame from birth, rose up, his feet and ankle bones received strength and he began 'walking and jumping, and praising God'. The powers-that-be demanded to know how Peter and John had healed the man, and they replied, 'It is by the name of Jesus Christ of Nazareth, whom you crucified but whom God raised from the dead' (Acts 4:10).

To call on the name of Jesus is enough to bring salvation and peace to anyone who repents of sin and asks for God's forgiveness.

Before the throne of God above
I have a strong and perfect plea.
A great high Priest, whose Name is Love,
Who ever lives and pleads for me.

My name is graven on His hands,
My name is written on His heart;
I know that while in Heaven He stands
No tongue can bid me thence depart.

When Satan tempts me to despair
And tells me of the guilt within,
Upward I look, and see Him there
Who made an end of all my sin.

Because the sinless Saviour died
My sinful soul is counted free.
For God the Just is satisfied
To look on Him and pardon me.

Behold Him there! The risen Lamb!
My perfect, spotless righteousness,
The great unchangeable I AM,
The King of Glory and of Grace.

One in Himself, I cannot die.
My soul is purchased by His blood,
My life is hid with Christ on high,
With Christ my Saviour and my God!

Charitie Lees Bancroft (1841-1923)

# 3

# Enough
# in Emotional Support

---

**Can God cope with someone's
loneliness and fearfulness?**

*'In that day you will call Me "my husband":
you will no longer call Me "my Master".*

*'I will betroth you to Me forever;
I will betroth you in righteousness and justice,
in love and compassion.
I will betroth you in faithfulness
and you will acknowledge the Lord.'*

Hosea 2:16, 19, 20

---

# |3|

# Enough
# in Emotional Support

Singleness is obviously a problem for many girls, no less on the mission fields than at home. We all have a need for companionship, someone to chat with and share problems with. During the war months, just to have someone else about was a comfort. When I was taken by those rebel soldiers on my own, it was far harder to cope than when we were all in a group and had each other around us. When I was sick and unable to look after myself, there were moments when I felt it would have been easier to cope had someone else been alongside.

Then the load of responsibilities. Medically, making decisions every day – diagnosing what was wrong, choosing how to treat the situation, preparing for operations and deciding the optimal moment for proceeding. When there was only enough of a particular medicine to treat one person and two people needed it, who should be treated? Who should not? It was especially difficult to decide when the one not treated would probably die and might have lived if treated.

Responsibilities of caring for a growing village – nursing students, often married and with small children; builders for the hospital and the church, and their wives and children; the many patients in the wards, and their helpers, needing feeding as well as housing. I had to learn how to make and burn bricks for all the needed constructions; I had to learn to barter for food supplies at local markets; I had to have time to prepare for preaching twice on Sundays, and for teaching daily in the Bible Study hour.

There were moments when my heart cried out to God, 'Why don't you send someone to help me?' As I have already said, it wasn't honestly a desire to be married, to have a husband, but a great longing to have someone alongside, to share the responsibilities and the work-load.

Then, during my first furlough, I was lying in a hospital bed, apparently dying, though no specific diagnosis had been made. I was overwhelmingly tired. My mother was told that the doctors were not very hopeful of my making a recovery. This news went round to the many friends who prayed for me – among them, my younger sister, a nun in a contemplative order of Anglican sisters. Diana asked permission of the Mother Superior to write me a letter and the nuns prayed for my recovery in their daily prayers.

A letter came from Diana and was sitting unopened among others on the locker beside the bed. A young student nurse was deeply distressed to see me so lethargic that I did not even open my letters. As she was going off duty, she called into the room where I lay and stood by my bed praying for me. She then picked up the top letter on the pile and opened it, so that she could read it to me. It was my younger sister's. In the letter, Diana quoted Hosea 2:16. The nurse turned to pick up my Bible and find the verse to read it to me.

'In that day,' declares the LORD, 'you will call me "my husband"; you will no longer call me "my master"' (Hosea 2:16).

Even in my lethargy, I remembered the verse and, even before the nurse read it to me, the word from God was working in my heart. God had spoken to me. 'Can you not trust me to be the companion you so long for? Am I not sufficient to supply your need, as your constant helper?'

And from that moment – to the amazement of the doctors – I began to get better.

Later, I read verse 16 in its context.

'Therefore I am now going to allure her; I will lead her into the desert and speak tenderly to her. There I will give her back her vineyards, and will make the Valley of Achor a door of hope' (Hosea 2:14, 15).

And further on, in verses 19-20,

'I will betroth you to me forever; I will betroth you in righteousness and justice, in love and compassion. I will betroth you in faithfulness, and you will acknowledge the LORD' (Hosea 2:19-20).

What wonderful promises. Perhaps the phrase that really stood out to me after I had read and meditated on the passage two or three times was 'The valley of Achor a door of hope.' The valley of Achor was where Achan sinned, after the victory of Jericho, when he stole silver and clothing. He was punished with a horrible death (Joshua 7:24-26).

But now, by God's grace, that very place becomes 'a door of hope' for Hosea's errant wife. I clutched at the truth in this wonderful statement – that the valley of Achor (the place of sinning) could become a door of hope (entrance into a new situation) by repentance – acknowledging again Jesus as my Saviour and Lord.

Eventually, I returned to the Congo with those words from Hosea beautifully carved for me on a wooden plaque: 'The valley of Achor – a door of hope!' Yes, God was sufficient. I did not *need* anyone else.

Four years later, on my second furlough, having been rescued from guerrilla soldiers and from five months of captivity in what came to be known as the Simba Uprising, I took many meetings up and down the UK to testify to the all-sufficiency of the grace of God. Even in the midst of unimaginable cruelty and suffering and danger, his grace was sufficient for each of us. His promise in Isaiah 26:3 – to keep us in perfect peace as our minds were stayed on him – was amazingly true.

I used to say, 'When your back's to the wall, He is sufficient for you. You need nothing else – just to keep your eyes fixed on Jesus!'

Seven years later, having gone back with many others and having worked hard to re-create all that had been destroyed, to start the college again and upgrade the standards every year, there was suddenly an uprising of students against authority, apparently saying that we (in particular, me) had embezzled college funds. I was devastated. There were no college funds – just generous gifts from supporters back in the UK. Everything that came month by month was ploughed into the work.

There followed a very painful 'trial'. The leaders of the medical centre sat as judge; the students were allowed to present their case. I was in the dock, as the accused. It was hard to believe that it was all actually taking place.

After having given all one had for twenty years, it had come to such a climax. Eventually I left and went up to my home in tears. What should I do next?

I took my Bible and sat down to pray. The marker was in Jonah (I was reading through the Bible in a year, and that was to be that day's reading.) I read through Jonah. It said nothing to me. I cried out to God to help me, 'Please, speak to me!' I read again through Jonah. God seemed silent. I started to read for the third time and as I read again through chapter one – of the wild storm at sea as Jonah sought to flee from God – it was suddenly so clear. Not only did Jonah and the people in the ship with him suffer from the storm – but also any other ships in the area would have been affected. God sent that storm to speak to Jonah but so many others were also affected.

This storm in the nurses' college – with all the students 'on strike' and no nurses at work in the hospital – was all because God wanted to speak to me!

God seemed to ask me a question.

'When you were at home after the rebellion, you told everyone that I, God, was sufficient for all your needs. Is that not still true?'

'Yes, God. Of course you are sufficient for all my needs.'

'No,' God seemed to reply, 'you want "Jesus plus". Plus a sense of success: going home with photographs of your students (and the football team you had coached); with tape recordings of the choir you had trained, singing parts of Handel's Messiah. You want the leadership to write to urge you to return again because they can't really cope with the college without you.'

My heart ached. A battle was raging inside me. Yes, I did want to be missed. Yes, I did need others to think of me as a success. Yet, at the same time, my heart knew that Jesus was all I actually wanted or needed.

At last, broken-hearted, I confessed to God my pride, and told him 'Yes, I only want Jesus – not "Jesus plus".'

The dear Lord restored peace to my heart, as once again he made so clear to me that Jesus is enough for every situation. His grace is sufficient to meet every need.

Evelyn Booth-Clibborn (grand-daughter of General Booth who founded the Salvation Army) captured this truth beautifully in one of her many hymns:

Peace, peace, God-given peace,
Deep in my soul doth abide;
Though pain and care I must know,
Jesus is near at my side.
*All that I need, all that I need,*
*Jesus, dear Lord, Thou art all that I need.*

Grace, grace, wonderful grace,
Freely Thou givest to me;
Grace for each test that may come,
If I but take it from Thee.

Hope, hope, radiant hope –
Soon all dark shadows must flee.
Then with what joy, full, complete,
I shall be ever with Thee.

© Evelyn Booth-Clibborn, 1965

# 4

# Enough
# to please God

---

'Thanks be to God,
Who always leads us in triumphal
procession in Christ
and through us, spreads everywhere
the fragrance of the knowledge of Him.
For we are to God the aroma of Christ ...'

'Who is equal *(sufficient)* for such
a task?'

'Not that we are competent *(sufficient)*
in ourselves
to claim anything for ourselves,
but our competence *(sufficiency)* comes
from God.'

2 Corinthians 2:14, 15 and 16, and 3:5
(Wording from the Authorised Version in brackets)

---

# | 4 |

# Enough
# to please God

HOW CAN I POSSIBLY PLEASE GOD?
Paul's standard for us, as he writes it to the
Corinthian church, is amazing. Certainly,
humanly, it seems quite out of reach – that
my life should be as the aroma of Christ to
all who meet with me. As the years march
past, I am increasingly conscious of what is
euphemistically called 'growing old', and with
it comes the realisation of how far short I fall
of the Biblical standard of Christ-likeness.

Only this could possibly issue in an aroma, a fragrance of Jesus. I find myself longing, more and more, that I should know him more clearly, follow him more nearly and, above all, love him more dearly – collectively that could bring forth 'an aroma of Christ'.

Each year, in the week between Christmas and New Year, I ask the Lord for a verse to guide me through the incoming new year. Two or three years ago, the Lord led me to Ephesians 1:17, 'I keep asking that the God of our Lord Jesus Christ, the glorious Father, may give you (me) the Spirit of wisdom and revelation, so that you (I) may know him better.' And how true that is. I just long to know him better – and thus to become more like him in every aspect.

Then we read of Paul's prayer when he was imprisoned in Rome, after years of missionary service, in his letter to the Philippians, 'I want to know Christ' (Phil. 3:10). But Paul knew Christ. He knew him wonderfully and intimately, he had been walking with Jesus for many years and serving him in all sorts of circumstances. What did he mean by this prayer, 'I want to know Christ'?

Is this not a common experience to most of us? The longer we walk with him, in some mysterious way, we seem to know him less and less clearly. And so comes the deep longing to know him better, to know him more deeply, more consistently, to know him in a manner that passes all understanding, 'to know him'.

Another year, the Lord laid Psalm 27:4 on my heart: 'One thing I ask of the LORD, this is what I seek: that I may dwell in the house of the LORD all the days of my life, to gaze upon the beauty of the LORD and to seek him in his temple.' What a wonderful picture that is. I had the verse written out on a card by my bedside, and I read it and prayed it daily throughout that year.

More and more, I have come to realise that love for my dear Lord and Saviour has to displace all other loves. Nothing else really counts. I must allow his love so to possess me that anything that hurts him hurts me. Equally, anything and everything that he loves, I am happy to love equally. But, even knowing this fact, I found it was not easy to let go of all else. At that moment in my life, someone gave me Jerry Bridges' book *Respectable Sins*. (Could there be such a thing – a respectable sin?) Chapter by chapter as

I went through this book, I came more and more under conviction. Things I had never thought of as sin, things that I perhaps called 'weaknesses', or 'not the best' – but not sin. Attitudes of heart that grieved God – my impatience with others, my irritability when others seemed so slow to see things as I saw them, my quickness to criticise another.

There is a chapter in the book on anxiety and frustration. Paul says to the Philippians, 'Do not be anxious about anything' (Phil. 4:6). Jesus himself gives a whole section of his Sermon on the Mount to this subject. 'Do not worry' is repeated three times in a few verses (Matt. 6:25-34). I worry – about everything and anything (some would say, 'Yes, and even about nothing!') But if the words of Jesus mean anything, they are a command to us not to worry. So worrying is a sin.

The same with the command not to be anxious at any time or in any circumstances. I could say that I am an anxious person by temperament. Just going out locally with a shopping list, I can manage to be anxious. Will I forget something? Have I enough money? Then to be challenged to realise that to be anxious is a sin, I found this almost overwhelming, certainly deeply uncomfortable. Bridges' chapters on discontentment and un-thankfulness were equally challenging, almost devastating. Where had I been all these years? Had I lived with my head in the sand, unwilling to call sin *sin* and therefore making no effort to bring each situation to God and to ask for forgiveness and deliverance?

Recently, I had to have surgery for cataracts and I found myself fearful and anxious, worrying about anyone touching my eyes without a general anaesthetic! I quoted, 'Cast all your anxiety on him because he cares for you' (1 Pet. 5:7) to myself, but it didn't bring me release from my fear. During one night the week before the first operation, I woke in the early hours to hear, as it were, the same verse spoken to me, only with a difference: 'Cast all your anxiety on *me*, for *I* care for you.' I was awed. The fear went. The anxiety disappeared. And I went through both operations at peace. Then – and from then, until today – I personally know that he has enough grace and power to enable us at every turn of events to rest in him, to trust him, and so to please him.

Bridges gives a chapter to the sin of hidden pride – moral superiority, self-righteousness, how we feel happy and content that we do not get caught up in open moral sin such as adultery, drunkenness or avarice. We can feel deeply distressed at the way our societies are going. We can even feel disgust at some of the horrific items we hear on the news, where other members of our society act in ways that are truly abhorrent to us. But is our initial reaction, 'There but for the grace of God go I'? Does what I have just heard lead me into prayer – for the individuals involved, for our degenerate society? Or am I content to be correct myself and critical of the others? Instead of rejoicing in God's goodness to me that has defended me from that particular sin, I take pride in my own ability to avoid the wrong (oh, the subtlety of pride, spiritual pride, pride in myself) rather than giving thanks to God for his amazing grace and for how he has delivered me from falling into that particular temptation.

There is the danger of reacting with pride when invited to speak at certain events, especially well-known events, of pride on being told the 'illustrious' names of those who have recently spoken at the same meeting and how many thousands are expected to

attend! Then there is the danger of the 'numbers game'. On one occasion, I was invited
by telephone to go to speak at a church conference in the USA near Chicago. I was told
'there will be six or seven thousand students
there'. I had already accepted an invitation to
a small local meeting of women on the same
date. I cancelled this and went to the USA.
Actually, I had misheard what was said to
me on the telephone: there were barely 600
young people at the conference! And it was
soon evident that they did not really want the
message that I believed God would have me
give. I had fallen for the numbers game. This
is simply pride – thinking one is capable of
the big event.

All these things in our lives must certainly
prevent us being a sweet aroma of Christ,
and certainly cause us not to be pleasing to
God – which I long to be with all my heart.
But can he change the picture? Has he the
power to enable us to give all these attitudes
to him and to allow the Holy Spirit to deal
honestly and truly with all that displeases
him? I am not really asking 'Has he enough
power to do what needs to be done in me?'
but rather, 'Have I enough grace and humility

to acknowledge what I need and to allow him to make the necessary change?' Yet I know that the needed grace and humility are his. And he certainly has enough of both to fulfil my need.

There are lots of similar temptations to those mentioned by Jerry Bridges, such as the desire to be recognised, to be thanked. Lack of self-control, my irritability towards another driver on the road who flashes his head-lights in a desire to pass when I am all set to turn right at the next exit. A quick retort when someone corrects me, as I feel, unjustly. I get impatient with people who tend to wait till the last minute to do things when I prefer to be unnecessarily early – such as going to church on Sundays or getting to the airport in time for a particular flight. There are probably many others of these so-called 'respectable sins' and each one needs to be brought to the cross and forgiveness sought.

The wonder is that God has put up with all these sins (failings, weaknesses) in me for a long time and is still patiently drawing me to himself and offering to change my very nature, so that it will become Christ-like. That is the ministry for which God sent us the

Holy Spirit – to make us holy, holy through and through, not just on the surface or in the eyes of others, but deep down inside, as he himself sees us. Praise be to God, that he has enough patience and love to go on making me into what he wants me to be – an aroma of Christ.

> Let the beauty of Jesus be seen in me,
> All his wondrous compassion and purity:
>     O Thou Spirit Divine,
>     All my nature refine,
> 'Till the beauty of Jesus be seen in me.

Albert Osborn

# 5

# Enough for Happiness and Contentment

---

**Do I sense that I need *something* – *something* MORE than I have in the Gospel – to be content? to be happy?**

*'I have learned to be content whatever the circumstances.*
*I know what it is to be in need,*
*and I know what it is to have plenty.*
*I have learned the secret of being content in every situation,*
*whether well-fed or hungry,*
*whether living in plenty or in want.*
*I can do everything through Him who gives me strength.'*

Philippians 4:11-13

---

# | 5 |

# Enough
# for Happiness
# and Contentment

In 2008, I became ill with polymyalgia which involved much pain and weakness. I was suddenly unable to look after myself. In fact, I was totally dependent on my friend for even the basic needs of life.

I soon realised that I was *not* content and I was finding it almost impossible to give thanks to God. This brought confusion to my mind. I knew the Scriptures clearly that told me to be content and give thanks in all situations, whatever the circumstances.

Paul, languishing in a prison cell and expecting death at any moment, wrote that 'I have learned to be content whatever the circumstances' (Phil. 4:11). In fact, he goes on in the next verse to say: 'I have learned the secret of being content in any and every situation, whether well fed or hungry, whether living in plenty or in want.' I simply wasn't there.

Not only was I not able to rejoice in the midst of the pain and weakness but, even more, I could not rejoice or give thanks in my utter dependence on my friend. It wasn't that she was unwilling to help me – not at all – but I knew I was using up her precious time. I felt I was imposing on her goodness.

Through those weeks (in fact, during the next year or so), I looked back over all my Christian life and I became conscious that God had tried to teach me to be willing to be dependent on others, on many occasions. When I was ill in Congo and African-trained paramedics cared for me, treated the cerebral malaria and nursed me back to life, I had to thank them – sincerely thank them – for all they had done for me. It was a reversal of roles – normally they thanked me for all I did for them but now I had to thank them.

And God was saying to me, 'This is necessary. They need to know that they are needed and that therefore they are fully part of the family.'

But I was so slow to learn the principle involved in this – the reversal of roles. I thought, as the foreign western missionary, it was right that they should acknowledge that they needed me. But that I, when sick and unable to cope, needed them so that they realised that they also were needed – that was a new angle and I was not altogether happy to adapt to it.

In the process, I certainly found it hard to be thankful or content. And now, some fifty years on, it was the same picture, though in a different setting.

God is so patient and kindly as he seeks to lead us on and teach us deeper truths. In the last few weeks, having been diagnosed as having cataracts, I was booked in to one of the local teaching hospitals for surgery. The first eye was 'done', and the result was wonderful. I could hardly believe the change – even colours looked brighter. But while the left eye could now focus without the help of spectacles, the right eye was

totally dependent still on the spectacles –
and the two eyes weren't working together.
Everything was 'wuzzy' and it meant that
I could not drive the car safely. So once more,
I was dependent on my friend for transport.
She willingly provided this but I was not
happy with the situation, knowing my needs
were disrupting her timetable.

Same problem – unwillingness to be dependent on another, however plausible my
reasoning as to why it was not fair on the
other person.

The 'wuzzy' sense of insecurity and the fear
of falling over or bumping into things – I was
not content with the situation, and I was not
being thankful to God, even though the first
operation had been a wonderful success. And
there was no reason to suppose the second operation would not be an equal success (which
it was). I should have been overwhelmingly
thankful to God: I live in an affluent western
country, with a well-organised health service
and adequately trained consultant ophthal-
mic surgeons available. In many developing
countries, these facilities are not yet in place.
I should have been thankful that I was able to
have operations. I should have been thankful

for all the amazing care given to us patients by the staff in the hospitals – everything was made so easy for us.

When I stopped to think like this and to reason rationally, I was indeed thankful to God. And the Lord restored to me a real sense of contentment in his plan for my life, no matter how dependent I had to be on another, no matter what pain or weakness accompanied the journey onwards. I was both thankful, and content, to be his child and in his care. He really was enough for happiness and contentment.

After all, did he not say, 'I have come that they may have life, *and have it to the full*' (John 10:10)?

Dear Jesus, make Thyself to be
A living, bright reality;
More present to faith's vision keen
Than any outward object seen:
More dear, more intimately nigh
Than e'en the sweetest earthly tie.

Charlotte Elliott (1789–1871)

# 6

# Our sufficiency is of God

---

'May the Grace of the Lord Jesus Christ
And the Love of God
And the Fellowship of the Holy Spirit
Be with you all.'

2 Cor 13:14

---

# | 6 |

# Our sufficiency
# is of God

WHAT IS IT THAT I REALLY NEED TO
GET ME THROUGH LIFE?
Grace, love and fellowship. What wonderful
words these are! Savour them.

'May the *grace* of the Lord Jesus Christ'–
in other words, all the unmerited favour that
God has poured upon me. I sometimes think
of the name of Jesus as being a synonym for
the word 'grace'. Paul wrote to Titus and said,
'the grace of God that brings salvation has
appeared to all men' (Titus 2:11). How did

God appear to all men? He appeared to us in and through Jesus, his beloved son. It is Jesus who reveals to us the Father's character, his love, his holiness – and, above all, his holy hatred of sin, sin that must be judged (as it says in Romans 6:23, 'The wages of sin is death.') And so we come to understand that the holy Son of God, born as the babe at Bethlehem, became flesh and dwelt among us in order that he might die in our place, as our substitute, our ransom. What a fantastic revelation of grace. And that grace, wholly revealed at the cross at Calvary, was sufficient to pay the price of all our sin. It was enough to pay the price of the sin of all people and of all time.

Jesus, suffering death upon the cross for our redemption, made there 'a full, perfect and sufficient sacrifice for the sins of the whole world'. These words from the Anglican Book of Common Prayer remind worshippers of the all-sufficiency of his death as they prepare for the Communion Service.

'May the *love* of God' – the love shed abroad in our hearts, poured out on us by the Holy Spirit. Immeasurable love, love that passes understanding, eternal love. Paul prayed for the young Christians in

Ephesus, that they might be strengthened with the power of the Spirit in their inner being, and become rooted and established in love, and so to grasp 'how wide and long and high and deep is the love of Christ, and to know this love that surpasses knowledge' (Eph. 3:18-19). What a prayer! A prayer that we might know something that 'surpasses knowledge', something so profound and overwhelming in its immensity that it cannot be known. Yet that is the love of God that he is willing to make known to us! And there is enough of that love of God to meet the needs of every human being throughout all ages. Enough and to spare!

'May the *fellowship* of the Holy Spirit' – the indwelling wonder of God's Spirit living in us, transforming us, making us daily more like Jesus (if we allow him to), causing us to hate sin and love everything that pleases God. What a tremendous truth. We are not left on our own, to stumble and trip up, to puzzle out the 'hows' and 'whys' of daily living. He is there as our friend and counsellor, our advocate and protector, our teacher and reminder of all we have been taught. He will never leave us, nor desert us. He is not fickle, nor does he show favouritism. He never grows weary and he is endlessly patient with us. His power to sanctify us has no limit; there is always enough of it for each one of us, each one of us who asks him to transform us into the likeness of the Lord Jesus.

How can we define that adjective 'enough' in a way that will help us to grasp the enormity of God's grace and love and fellowship? The sufficiency of God! I love the last verses of Ephesians 3: 'Now to him who is able to do immeasurably more than all we ask or imagine, according to his power that is at work within us, to him be glory in the church and in Christ Jesus throughout all generations, for ever and ever! Amen' (Eph. 3:20-21).

Wonderful! 'Immeasurably more than' is the best we can do to translate the super-abundant word in the Greek! It is a superlative of a superlative. It is beyond translation. It just sums up the entire and unquestionable sufficiency of God to meet our every need in every possible circumstance. That is to say, it expresses the 'enough' of God's grace and goodness.

Think of the story recorded in each of the four gospels where Jesus feeds the five thousand people gathered on the mountainside to listen to him teaching them throughout the daylight hours of the day.[1] Jesus had gone across the lake in a boat with his disciples to have a day apart from the crowds, for quietness and rest. But many saw him going and ran on foot to get there ahead of them. When Jesus saw the crowds, he was filled with compassion for them, and began to teach them many things. As the hours passed, the disciples tried to persuade him to send the crowd away, so they could buy food in the surrounding villages and towns.

Jesus challenged them saying, 'You give them something to eat.'

There were five thousand men there! Add to that possibly another five thousand women, and even five thousand children! How could the disciples ever give them enough, even for everyone to have a small bite, let alone to satisfy their hunger?

We know the story so well. The disciples found a lad in the crowd with his lunch – five small rolls and two sardines – and, somewhat wryly, they asked Jesus, 'Where will that go among so many?' (John 6:9)

---

1    This can be found in Matthew 14, Mark 6, Luke 9 and John 6.

Jesus took the loaves and fish, he blessed them, and broke them, and gave them to his startled disciples, and commanded them to distribute them to the vast crowd. They did so and everyone had all he needed to satisfy his hunger – and then the disciples gathered up twelve basketfuls of broken pieces of bread and fish.

Had there been enough? Yes, enough and to spare.

It is always the same with Jesus, he has 'enough and to spare' of grace, and love, and the power of his fellowship. He will never fail to give us all we need for absolute happiness and peace and contentment in him. Wonderful gospel!

As Paul asked, when the Holy Spirit challenged him (and, through him, all of us) to be as the aroma of Christ, the fragrance of life, 'Who is sufficient for these things?' And he answered, 'Not that we are sufficient of ourselves... But our sufficiency comes from God' (2 Cor. 2:16 & 3:5 AV).

Hallelujah! He has enough of everything I need. He is my sufficiency for every single day of my life, whatever it holds of joy or sorrow, blessing or challenge, of pleasure or pain.

He giveth more grace when the burdens grow greater,

He sendeth more strength when the labours increase;

To added affliction He addeth His mercy;

To multiplied trials, He multiplies peace.


When we have exhausted our store of endurance,

When our strength has failed ere the day is half done,

When we reach the end of our hoarded resources,

Our Father's full giving is only begun!


Fear not that thy need shall exceed His provision,

Our God ever yearns His resources to share;

Lean hard on the arm everlasting, availing;

The Father both thee and thy load will upbear.


His love has no limit, His grace has no measure,

His power has no boundary known unto men;

For out of His infinite riches in Jesus

He giveth, and giveth, and giveth again!


Annie Johnston Flint (1866-1932)

# Epilogue

What more can we say? Throughout the Bible, God draws the eyes of Christians forward to that wonderful time when we shall see him face-to-face, no longer darkly as in a mirror. Scripture only tells us a limited amount of the wonders of that time. So as we sing of it, we are seeking to express what we believe it will be like, to the best of our human comprehension.

There is a higher throne
Than all this world has known,

Where faithful ones from ev'ry tongue
Will one day come.
Before the Son we'll stand,
made faultless through the Lamb;
Believing hearts find promised grace;
Salvation comes.

*Hear heaven's voices sing;*
*Their thund'rous anthem rings*
*Through em'rald courts and sapphire skies;*
*Their praises rise.*
*All glory, wisdom, pow'r,*
*Strength, thanks and honour are*
*To God our King, who reigns on high*
*For evermore.*

And there we'll find our home;
Our life before the throne.
We'll honour him in perfect song
Where we belong.
He'll wipe each tear-stained eye
As thirst and hunger die.
The Lamb becomes our Shepherd-King;
We'll reign with him.

Keith and Kristyn Getty

In heaven, we will experience the ultimate
fulfilment of all that grace has made possible
for us, all that Christ's death on the cross of
Calvary bought for us – forgiveness of our

sins, peace of heart, friendship with God, the 'enough-ness' in every area of our lives that we have been thinking about.

And it has all been made possible through grace – made possible through Jesus, our beloved Saviour. Before Jesus came to Gethsemane and Calvary, he prayed to his Father, 'Father, glorify your name' and the Father replied, 'I have glorified it, and will glorify it again' (John 12:28.) Was the Father not referring to the cross, as being the moment in history when he would most clearly reveal to us his glory – when grace would be shown to us in all its fullness?

As I try to conceive of the fullness of grace, my mind moves to Titus 2:11, 'For the grace of God that brings salvation has appeared to all men.' He is talking of the Lord Jesus himself – he is the grace that brings salvation and has appeared to us all. And Paul goes on, 'we wait for the blessed hope – the glorious appearing of our great God and Saviour, Jesus Christ, who gave himself for us to redeem us from all wickedness' (Titus 2:13-14). One day, he will return.

As we experience, by grace, the great things that he has done for us here in our present life, it still remains largely beyond our ability to conceive of the wonders of heaven.

> No eye has seen,
> No ear has heard,
> No mind has conceived
> What God has prepared for those who love him (1 Cor. 2:9).

He promises that, on that day, there will be no more tears, no more pain, no more regrets, no more fears, no more mourning, no more death. All the human emotions and frailties that distract us now, all that causes us to feel less than content, everything that makes us other than happy and at peace – they will be no more. All that causes us now to seek to know the enoughness, the all-sufficiency, of his grace – they were part of a world that has now passed away. On that wonderful day, not only will there be no hindrance to true worship of our beloved Lord and Saviour (the negative aspect of the work of grace), but there will be an utter fulfilment of all that his grace has procured for us (the positive aspect). And more, there will be enough time to love him as we should, and to worship and serve him utterly as we long to do.

What a wonderful prospect!

So as we are learning now that God's grace and love and fellowship are indeed enough in this 'down-here' life, we are encouraged by all the wonderful promises for the life-to-come, the life 'up-there'. All God's promises, that we have watched being fulfilled here and now, will be finally completed when we are in his nearer presence.

In his vision, the Apostle John said:

> I saw a new heaven and a new earth ... I saw the Holy City ...

> He will wipe every tear from their eyes. There will be no more death or mourning or crying or pain, for the old order of things has passed away (Rev. 21:1-4).

But with that negative declaration of what there won't be in heaven, there came (first, actually) the wonderful positive truth of what there will be in heaven.

Now the dwelling of God is with men, and he will live with them. They will be his people and God himself will be with them and be their God (Rev. 21:3).

As we look forward with longing to that day, we can pray with John, 'Come, Lord Jesus' (Rev. 22:20).

*Now*, while we are still on earth, we can truly sing wholeheartedly the first three verses of John Newton's hymn:

Amazing Grace! How sweet the sound
That saved a wretch like me!
I once was lost, but now am found;
Was blind, but now I see.

'Twas grace that taught my heart to fear,
And grace my fears relieved;
How precious did that grace appear
The hour I first believed.

Through many dangers, toils and snares,
I have already come;
'Tis grace that brought me safe thus far,
And grace will lead me home.

But *then*, when we arrive in glory, we will truly experience that of which we sing in verse 4, the glorious freedom of worship – the enough-ness of time!

When we've been there ten thousand years,
Bright shining as the sun,
We've no less days to sing God's praise
Than when we first begun.

John Newton (1725-1807)

# About the Author

Dr Helen Roseveare went to Congo in 1953. She has dedicated her life to serving others even in the deep trials of life. She pioneered vital medical work in the rainforests of what is now the Democratic Republic of Congo, and is an internationally-respected speaker with W.E.C. ministries.

Some of her works include:

*Digging Ditches: The Latest Chapter of an Inspirational Life*
    (ISBN 978-1-84550-058-0)

*Give Me This Mountain*
    (ISBN 978-1-84550-189-1)

*He Gave Us a Valley*
    (ISBN 978-1-84550-190-7)

*Living Faith: Willing to be Stirred as a Pot of Paint*
    (ISBN 978-1-84550-295-9)

*Living Fellowship: Willing to be the Third side of the Triangle*
    (ISBN 978-1-84550-351-2)

*Living Holiness: Willing to be the Legs of a Galloping Horse*
    (ISBN 978-1-84550-352-9)

*Living Sacrifice: Willing to be Whittled as an Arrow*
    (ISBN 978-1-84550-294-2)

# Christian Focus Publications

## publishes books for all ages

Our mission statement –

STAYING FAITHFUL
In dependence upon God we seek to impact the world through literature faithful to His infallible Word, the Bible. Our aim is to ensure that the Lord Jesus Christ is presented as the only hope to obtain forgiveness of sin, live a useful life and look forward to heaven with Him.

REACHING OUT
Christ's last command requires us to reach out to our world with His gospel. We seek to help fulfil that by publishing books that point people towards Jesus and help them develop a Christ-like maturity. We aim to equip all levels of readers for life, work, ministry and mission.

Books in our adult range are published in three imprints:

*Christian Focus* contains popular works including biographies, commentaries, basic doctrine and Christian living. Our children's books are also published in this imprint.

*Mentor* focuses on books written at a level suitable for Bible College and seminary students, pastors, and other serious readers. The imprint includes commentaries, doctrinal studies, examination of current issues and church history.

*Christian Heritage* contains classic writings from the past.

# 10Publishing
## a division of 10ofthose.com

10Publishing is the publishing house of 10ofThose. It is committed to producing quality Christian resources that are Biblical and accessible.

www.10ofthose.com is our online retail arm selling 1000's of quality books at discounted prices. We also service many church bookstalls around the UK and can help your church to set up a bookstall. Single and bulk purchases welcome.

For more information contact: sales@10ofthose.com or check out the website: www.10ofthose.com